The Mountain Top
and other poems

Linda Hudson Hoagland

ISBN: 9798877656550

Victoria Fletcher
hootbookspublishing.biz
vfletcher56@gmail.com

Linda Hudson Hoagland

Contents

A NICE YOUNG MAN

His name was Nadine, a nice young man
the same age as me, he was my friend.
We talked as we swung in Lincoln Park.
A long summer was ended with him.

We both started school in the ninth grade.
I sought to speak to him to renew
the happy conversations we shared
swinging through hours innocent and free.

I saw him in the hallway and spoke.
My hand was pulled away by Karin,
"Don't speak to him," she harshly whispered.
"If you do, we will not be friends."

"Why," was all I managed to sputter,
not understanding the mean remark.
I needed to know why it was wrong.
"Puerto Rican," she hissed with venom.

I did as she said, forgetting him,
not claiming Nadine as my good friend.
To this day I am so sorry that
She taught me to hate the color of skin.

A VOYEUR'S LOOK

Booths that measure ten by ten
are filled with treasures that are
not sought by all but by those
who secretly know their measure.

Hand built wooden toys top the
table across from me to
delight the youngest to the
old who are gazing at them.

I am with writers of books
who capture history to
imaginings from active
minds telling of the people.

Some of those people fill the
future pages of those books
by making items by hand
that reflect the past culture.

Our culture and heritage
should always be remembered.
Use it to influence the
future of all who follow.

The Mistletoe Market is
a voyeur's vision at what
was, what is, and what will be
in our Appalachian life.

ADDIE

She's eighty-nine, a fossil by most
standards. Nonetheless, she is sharp, spry,
and willing to help any of her
friends. When I see that head of gray curls
bobbing up and down and walking toward
me, I'm happy to see her. I hope
that scene is repeated many times
because that's my lovely friend, Addie.

ALONE

Ev'ry day before my alarm rings,
long before the sun rises, I am up
ready to face my day. Breakfast
followed by reading, crocheting, or
writing is what I endeavor to
accomplish daily because I am
a widow and always home alone.
When I finally discover a
reason to leave the confines of my
house, I am out my front door— alone.

ALZHEIMER

My thoughts.

My memories.

All scrambled.

APPALACHIAN FUN

Whoops and hollers are shouted from the
inexperienced square dancers who
are out to have a fun filled time.
Appalachian life is there to be
enjoyed by one and all. Let's go to
the festival and have a good time.

BOOK 13

"Treat that book like it's made of gold,"
said my teacher as she handed
me my textbook. "If you lose it
or damage it, your parents will
have to pay for it." I looked the
book over reading the cover,
the back, and the spine which is the
part everyone sees when the
book is placed on a shelf. I did
want my name on that spine to show
all that I was a writer and
at that point in my young life, the
word author had not found its place
in my vocabulary, so
a writer was what I would be.
At the age of sixteen, I spent
hours writing and then rewriting
my novel. With encouragement
from only Mrs. Ruby, my
seventh grade teacher, I did not
show my finished product until
fifty years later. At that time
I was asked by Little Creek Books
to start a mystery series
for their imprint. After my first
Lindsay Harris Mystery was

published, I was asked if I had
anything else available.

I dusted off my first novel
and emailed it to her. It was
accepted immediately;
all I could think was, *Why didn't
I show it to someone sooner.*
It sat on the shelf for fifty
years because life got in the way.
The Best Darn Secret, my thirteenth
book published, but the first one I
ever wrote. Thank you Little Creek
Books for fulfilling a dream.

CALL OF KINDNESS

The death of my husband of twenty-five
years brought on loneliness and depression
for me to suffer through until I could
refocus my life and begin again.

My friend, Patty, knew that the evenings
were the most difficult for me to live
through without succumbing to dark thoughts.
She called every evening starting
with the day of my husband's funeral.

"Are you okay," she asked and I answered.
My reply was, "Fine." She would probe because
'fine' wasn't good enough. She knew the word
was whispered in passing to all of those
who didn't care but she wanted the truth.

Eight years have passed since that first phone call and
she calls almost every evening.
Those phone calls gave me a reason to heal and
wait for the next needed call of kindness.

ED – FATHER OF MY SONS

I thought I loved him with all my heart.
It didn't take long to discover
That I was so very, very wrong.
He really should have stayed a lover.

We married after a moment of love
And we thought it would last forever.
With a baby I was to become.
To deny it life I would never.

At the end of five long loveless years,
I decided we should surely part.
He fought me displaying pure spite
But there was no way to heal my heart.

FLAG OF FREEDOM

The flag was tattered and torn from
the relentless wind. I was not
the keeper of the flag pole but
I so much wanted to remove
the tatters and replace it with
a brand new flag I had squirreled
away for that special purpose.

My neighbor lowered the tattered
flag and removed the flag pole, too.

I gazed through my front window and
truly missed the reminder of
freedom that we should all take to
heart. I was so disappointed
with the absence of the flag that
I knew I had to do something
about the loss so I pulled out
the flag I sequestered, shoved it
into a plastic bag, and placed
it anonymously on my
neighbor's front porch. A couple of
years earlier I had offered
to give him a flag, but he would
not take it. I was sure he was
afraid there might be strings attached

to the gesture. By my placing
the flag on his porch secretly,

he might raise it up on his flag
pole. I watched and waited for the
flag and the flag pole to appear.

The flag of freedom is flying
gracefully on my street again.

FRIGID FULL MOON

The ice blue glimmer of the frigid full
moon hangs over our heads as we stare in
wonder at the cold beauty spread before us.
The ice caps and snow peaks of the mountains,
as dangerous as they may be, entice
the residents to assemble and pay
homage to their reason for survival.

GRANDMA WISHES

I watched as she reached into her
handbag. She was searching inside
in pursuit of a small photo
album. I had the opportunity
to ohhh and ahhh at the pictures
of grandchildren.

She had no idea how much
her proud display hurt my heart. My sons
did not find the need to create
offspring, thus my chance of being
a grandma disappeared.

The only thing within my grasp
to ohhh and ahhh at were photos of
someone else's grandbabies.

GRAY CROWNED ANGELS

Gray crowned angels fill the lobby
in front of the gift shop today.
Many here for a great hobby,
others need a good place to stay.

They are selling homemade items
baked and mixed to each one's delight.
Earning funds to purchase systems
for the staff to help fight the fight.

Several hours dedicated
without earning an hourly wage.
Helping all was for them fated
as they took turns working each day.

They give their time with love for all
they endeavor to help survive
the illness or unlikely fall.
They sell trinkets from nine to five.

The hospital is lucky to
have them working to earn the funds
to give them a helping hand to
buy things needed with well-earned funds.

HAPPY HELLO

The phone call,
I needed it.
It kept me
going each day
as I awaited
the familiar voice.

When Sonny died,
I was alone.
That was when
the calls started.

Loneliness wasn't so
all-consuming when
that phone rang
and I heard
the happy 'hello.'

HOMELESS

Left Turn Lucy should be my new name
because of my unchanging desire to
drive off into the wrong direction.
I did exactly that when I went in
search of the Harvest Table where I
could set up and sell the books I wrote.
I located the establishment
and exited my car where I went
in search of the person I needed
to talk with to get myself set up
and ready to sell. I started to
walk to the front of the building
and I spotted a walking, raggedy-
clothed man who was disheveled to the
point of needing a good hard scrubbing.
He was no more than five-two with long,
straggly gray hair, a dirty beard, and
moustache. From his shoulders he had tied
on cloth bags that seemed to be empty
waiting to be filled with whatever.
Initially I was frightened of
this small man but when he said "hello"
in a bright and cheerful tone, my first
impression changed. He appeared to
be homeless but not unhappy. He
didn't ask me for anything for

which I was relieved because that would
have caused my opinion of him
to be drastically different.

I believed he was on his way to
collect cans and other items that would earn
him some eating or drinking money.
If I hadn't been running late for
my commitment to set up and sell
my books, I would have loved to have talked
with him. I might have contributed
some funds to help him survive.

I ADORED MR. LACE

I adored Mr. Lace, not in the
man and woman way, but like when a
person truly admires another
human being. If Glen had asked me
to walk on hot coals, I would ask, "When?"

I was loyal and protective of
him and I would have defended him
to my death if the need arose since
I knew that he wouldn't or couldn't
mislead me or take advantage of
me with any malicious intent.
We understood and liked each other.
We truly respected the other.

Glen was Vice President in charge of
sales and was covered with paperwork
that didn't allow him to visit
customers as he should have or deal
directly with their many problems.

It was decided by the powers
above Glen on the food chain that the
company lacked a sales manager.
Feelers were issued and Lester Wilcox

was the man Glen hired. "You've just hired your
replacement," I whispered to Glen when
he proudly introduced me to him.

"No, no, Ellen, he's the Outside Sales
Manager. That's all," he explained.
I shook my head and walked away with
a rock positioned in my stomach.

Glen was truly a good man. He was
soft spoken and kind-hearted, so if
any of his employees approached
him with a reasonable sob story,
he would believe the tale he was told.

Glen didn't see through those rose colored
glasses; his world was highlighted
by the glorious shade of rose red.
Within two months, Glen was asked to leave.
Wilcox was to be his replacement.
My prediction had come true.
Glen took the news with much grace and grit.
I heard the sad news and vowed vengeance.

The next time I saw Glen, he mentioned
to me that he had just seen Wilcox.
He explained further that Wilcox told
him of the revenge I had followed.

Lester Wilcox had assumed with his
promotion that he had acquired free
reign to do to his new employees
whatever and whenever he pleased.

His method for sorting through females
for possible promotion was to
test them between the sheets— I wouldn't
do that for any job promotion
so I proceeded to let those in
the tower of power know my thoughts.

Glen called me and told me about a
job opening in his company.
When I was assured of being hired,
I started the wheels in motion and left.
Wilcox was fired just two weeks later.

Upon seeing me again, Glen smiled
and said, "I'm glad I never made you
angry enough to get your revenge."
My response, "I didn't get revenge,
I got even."

I AM AN AUTHOR

I am a writer, an author, a scribe
of words and tales. It was a difficult
phrase for me to say above a whisper.
"I am an author."
I have finally accepted that as truth.
I wanted to share my gift with others.
About five years ago, I volunteered
to teach a group of older students to
begin their journey into writing at
the College for Older Adults in the
Town of Abingdon, Virginia, where
one of my former students sent me a signed
copy of his published book. I continued
to volunteer teach there for three years which
was located about fifty miles from
my home; but, I wanted to encourage
my neighbors and friends on getting started
into the wonderful world of writing.
Southwest Virginia Community
College allowed me to encourage the
local students to take that writing trip.
I have had the honor of encouraging
seven students as a volunteer for
a semester where I know one of the
students will become a debut published
writer with a second student closely

following his lead. I hope I can push
my students to publication success
and I hope that I can afford to do
so on a volunteer basis— because I am an author.

I FINALLY GOT IT RIGHT

Marriage, divorce, struggle to survive
with two small sons hanging on for life.
I plunged into an unhappy life
followed by divorce. Number three was
good and I finally got it right.
Twenty-five years later, I was a
widow. No more climbs up that mountain
because the trip down is too painful.

I WILL ALWAYS REMEMBER

He tucked the money away as he
looked around suspiciously, as
if many men were gathered on the
stairway behind him waiting for the
chance to turn him upside down shaking
him until his pockets were emptied
but that was how he always acted
after the accident. He had been
diagnosed having paranoia
that probably would never completely
go away.

"Eddy, come on, these people are your
friends," Ellen, his mom, whispered to him.
Eddy wanted so much to tell her
the truth. Some were his friends, a few; but
most of them were there to grab what they
could get their hands on and he knew that
was the truth— not paranoia.
"Watch them, mom," he whispered. "I'll tell you
about some of them later. You really
can't trust them."

Eddy tried to smile and be friendly
which was totally contrary to
his post-accident behavior.

After everyone left, after he
had carefully searched them with his eyes,
he told his mother what had happened
on previous visits.
"Some of them took my cassettes, my good
ones, and said that I gave them away.
When I asked for them to be returned,
I never got them back, and I will
always remember who I can't trust."
"Why didn't you tell me about this
sooner," Ellen asked. "They would deny
it because I'm a crazy paranoid."
He wasn't so crazy.

JOE – MY WORK LOVE

Chains of gold around his neck.
Gold-rimmed glasses on his eyes.
Fringes of long leather straps
Hang loose fluttering like flies.

Hair of dark brown, straight and true.
To his broad shoulders it hangs.
His mustache is trimmed and neat
Beneath his even cut bangs.

That is the look for the show.
He plays a guitar so fine.
He plans to become famous
Then he'll mellow like fine wine.

I met him at work each day
Dressed like all those around him:
Jeans and a tattered tee shirt
Until music sounds call him.

JOHN – MY DANGEROUS LOVE

We met in a blue collar bar.
I was searching for the unknown:
A new friend with whom I could spend
A short time of talking alone.

He was the tender of all drinks:
Beer, shot, and mixed drinks were all served.
Coke and ginger-ale in glasses.
Trust him we did until we were perturbed.

It seems he added some white pills
To my glass to spread his feeling
To me and make me share his happy,
Not my sad; it was not healing.

I must have sensed his doing
A destructive misdeed to me.
I threw glasses and chairs at him
And from him I was forced to flee.

JUSTICE

"Those are the sandals that were left on
the sand after my daughter was kidnapped
by God," said a distraught mother as
she was being questioned by the man
who was trying to convict her dead
daughter's murderer— ten years later
she was questioned by an aggressive
and heartless newspaper reporter.

My daughter's feet will never again
fill the sandals that were left on that
lonely beach. Her killer will never
ever be able to walk on the
same stretch of that lovely beach again.

Linda Hudson Hoagland

LEAVES TUMBLE

The air was crisp forcing faces to glow
crimson with people searching for comfort
from heat to stop the sparkly tears that flow
streaking down cheeks with wiping an effort.

The dry, brittle leaves begin to tumble,
flitting, flying, twisting end over end
hitting the hard ground with not a rumble,
preparing the world for the message to send.

The green grass shone from a clear coat of ice,
crunching underfoot bringing out reminders
of seasons gone by. Most of them were nice
but falling, sliding, and wearing blinders

prevents me from enjoying the splendor
before me with the colorful grandeur.

LIVE

The dark clouds
are swirling around
beginning to break
up and disappear.

We can go
meet and greet
all of those
we have avoided.

The prospect of
death and dying
has weighed heavily
on everyone.

Maybe we all
will get through
this trouble and
live our lives.

MAYBE

"What was that," asked Melanie as she
pointed to a strange sight outside of
her kitchen window that caused her stare.
"What are you talking about," asked her
skeptical husband of many years.
"Look at it for yourself, why don't you?"
He walked slowly, rubbing at his eyes.
"What's happening to my itchy eyes?"
"There is something green growing up where
the snow and ice used to be," she said.
"Is it gone," he asked rubbing his eyes.
"Is what gone," she said questioning him.
"The snow and ice, has it gone away?"
"Yes, there is nothing but brown outside
and a beautiful, bright, blue sky."
"Where did it go? What happened to it?"
"Melted and totally disappeared."
"How? It's not warm enough to melt it."
"Well, the air has been warmer the last
few months; and it is all really gone."
"What now," he asked. He was so perplexed
with this development that had not
occurred since he was a little child.
"Just wait and see what happens. In the
meantime, look at that green thing. You can
almost see it reaching for the sun."

"Is the world coming to an end? The
scientists have said that if all of the
snow melts, the world as we know it will
come to an end," he said solemnly.
"No, no, this is a new beginning.
I looked it up on the computer
and that little plant is a crocus.
It's the first sign of spring that we've had
in fifty years. We need to enjoy
the new green life to bloom before us."

MAYBE

MEETING AND GREETING

My eyes opened with a start.
It was Sunday; my day, once
again, to try to sell my
books I had written to those
who expressed an interest.
I'm a regional writer
who looks forward to meeting
and greeting people. I smiled
to all comers and then I said,
"Do you like to read?"

MIKE – MY SECOND ATTEMPT

He was a wonderful man
With two daughters of his own.
He treated me very fine.
Love for me was always shown.

The children: my sons, his girls,
Promised to share our joined lives
In peace and tranquility.
In fact, the promise was lies.

I chose to end the joining,
Not to look back in regret.
My sons and I did move on
And a new sail we did set.

MUD TRACKS

"Follow the mud tracks," Susan shouted
to Annie as she pointed to the
vinyl covered floor. They both tiptoed
and whipped their heads side to side searching
for the uninvited visitor.
"It's got to be here. I saw it as
it slid over the threshold," she said.
"Right there," screamed a panicky Annie.

Snake!

MY BAD

Fabric squares, not perfect but sewn by hand
with special care to save many moments
of my and mother's lives into a band
making them appear to be monuments.

I spread the handmade quilt across my bed
to give me the warmth and comfort I sought.
Much to my dismay it filled me with dread
because of all of the nightmares it brought.

Not all squares represented good life tales.
Those that were bad came to the very front
into my dreams with all of its big sails,
the ship destroyed my sleep with its affront.

Not all memories are good, some are bad.
From the quilt my bad replays can be had.

MY BIG BROTHER

Sharp was not a word to describe Terry.
He was a bully, hard to get along
with, and unfriendly. With that said, I don't
want you to say anything bad about
him. He struggled through life for seventy
three years alone, most of the time, of his
own choosing. I miss my big brother.

MY CARD

"Here, officer, you need to see this,"
I said as I held up my get out
of jail free card. "Sorry, ma'am. This is
the one I have that will trump your card.

GO DIRECTLY TO JAIL

DO NOT PASS GO

DO NOT COLLECT $200

You were doing seventy in a
thirty five zone."

MY HUSBAND – MY HERO

He fought so hard to stay with me,
To help me get through day to day.
His medicines and physicians
drained me of each hard earned payday.

I don't regret one cent paid
to stave off the approach of death.
Time after time he struggled
to come back home with me to rest.

A simple procedure cost him
because his heart could take no more.
He never awoke to find out
how much more pain he had in store.

He is my hero for fighting
The fight to make it through each bout
Of poking, prodding, and guessing.
His problem was always in doubt.

MY SECRET TRIP

I crouched down as far as my ten year old
legs would allow me as I crawled
along the deep ditch to get past my
daddy's garden. I had to slip off
from home so I could get into the
back of a red pickup truck with the
members of the junior camera
club and take a hundred mile plus trip
to Camden Park. I didn't have much
money but I knew I could get on
a ride or two. I could get something
to eat and then come home to slip back
into the house and smile about my
secret trip. My mom knew I had gone
on the trip. I didn't tell her but
she knew. Neither of us told daddy
because I would have been in a lot
of trouble. To this day, I smile when
I think of riding in the back of
that red pickup truck with my friends.

NEIGHBOR ENVY

She is close to ninety and has
a speaking disability.
She does have many family
members who care. I can see car
after car with passengers who
enter her welcoming house, staying
for a short while and leave. As that
car leaves the driveway, another
one enters with a warm welcome.

I get to see my sons rarely,
even though my youngest tells all
who ask that he returned to my
small town from his Nebraska home
to take care of me. I might see
him once every couple of
weeks. My eldest son works in a
coal mine with a solitary
life until he met a lady
that swept him off of his feet. His
time was spent with her until she
ended the relationship due
to the distance between their homes.
Even though he is alone, I
might see him once a month.

Both sons live less than ten miles from
my house. The mileage grows and grows
with each passing day.

My neighbor sees her family
members daily but even though
I suffer from neighbor envy,
I continue to love my sons
with all I have in me.

NOT IN OUR BED

She looked at me with disdain
etched on her face so I'd see
her dislike of me was plain.
Acceptance was not to be.

I was a southern woman,
Virginia born and bred so
I did not fit her big plan.
So she wanted me to go.

A Polish, Catholic girl
Was her choice for her first son.
Protestant was not the pearl
in the oyster for her son.

Nevertheless, we did wed
despite her strong objections.
Her choices, not in our bed,
As we fought her rejections.

OLD

Spring arrives
with sunshine.
Don't care.

Family doesn't
check mom.
She's old.

Alone and
dead for
two weeks.

Tomorrow is
not known
for all.

PANIC

"Take out a blank sheet of paper
and a pencil. Put all other
items beneath your desk and do
it now," said Mrs. Smith as she
lifted the chalkboard eraser
and approached the big blackboard that
held the explanation for the
reason for the panic that was
filling my fast fluttering heart.

PROUD PEACOCK

The black comb was pulled from his pocket so
he could run it through his pompadour-styled
dark blonde hair. He preened as he awaited
the appearance of the female bird he
planned to sweep off of her feet and convince
her of his undying love for only
that one night stand.

PUBLISHED OPINES

I saw an article in McCall's
entitled "Between Friends" that would pose
three questions each month to readers
who were invited to submit their
opinions and receive a tidy
sum of fifty dollars per published
answer. I always prided myself
in my ability to write about
any ordinary life subject
you could name. I wouldn't delve into
scientific matters for which I
had no expertise, but on about
any other subject I could have
a pro or con position. I would
make monthly trips to the library
where I would browse through the magazine
looking for questions that I felt I
could answer without embarrassing
myself too much. The editors asked
the public who supplied the answers
to submit their name or withhold their
name to avoid bald embarrassment.
I wasn't ashamed of any of
my answers. As a matter of fact,
I was happy that they thought enough
of my answers to even read them.

The first letter I had published in
January of '96 was
about a person who was more than
generous with her gifts to others
who felt they were unable to do
the same and thought that perhaps they should
refuse to accept the gift. I answered
that I knew the poverty feeling
well but I have learned to accept the
fact that my friend is a generous
person to be accepted 'as is.'
Just as she has learned to welcome my
handmade items I had invested
many long hours into creation.
Our friendship is much too valuable
to allow any doubt to shatter it.
Three years later, I responded to
a letter about curbing the rights
of smokers to puff around children.
As a former smoker, I know what
it's like to be told that you must leave
the room to do something that you had
been doing freely a couple of years
earlier; but, with all of the health
news— discoveries about second
hand smoke being harmful to those near,
I feel that the couple has a right
to say no and ask the smoker to
leave the room. The hard, hurt feelings will

fade if the friendship is worth saving.
Two years passed and I opined about
a lonely wife who missed family
and friends when she was forced to move on
because of her husband's job. It seems
that the husband would not let his wife
take trips home to visit family
and friends. My idea was that she
should fill her lonely hours by going
out of the house and forcing herself
to make new friends and visit places
so she could also start a new life.
Limit her visits back home as her
husband requested and don't allow
herself to be forced into choosing
between her previous life and spouse.
Fortunately I earned a total of
one hundred fifty dollars for a
span of five years and couldn't have been
happier with the results. I haven't
come across any other magazines
who are willing to pay me for my
opinions, but if I do, I will
submit them with the thought that they might
be worth something to somebody and
not only the editor who has
chosen my opinion to publish.

RAISING THE BAR, AGAIN

The closet in the dining room was the
place of choice to hide my written stories.
I would carry my spiral-bound notebook
crammed in my school books so no one, teacher
or fellow student, would know that what I
worked on diligently was not homework
assigned to me by any of my teachers,
but flights of fancy as created by
my overactive imagination.

My desire, perhaps I should say dire need,
manifested itself in my mind when
I attended elementary school.
Story books would be handed to each of
us with the admonition that we must
take special care of the books and never
cause the binding to crack and break because
that was the way the books were located
when perched on shelves awaiting perusal.

I wanted my name on that binding. I
knew that sounded a little silly but
that was my choice. The only way I was
going to get my name on that binding
was to write a book of my own. It began.
I carried a notebook, filled it with words.

I would become discouraged with writing
and the lack of any encouragement.
The feeling of futility would cause
me to swear off ever writing again,
hide my words in the dining room closet.
That would last about a week. I was back
at the words until I decided I
had enough and into the closet the
writings would be safely placed once again.

When I graduated from high school, life
seemed to get in my way preventing me
from ever achieving my writing goal.
I lived through many experiences
I knew could and should be the beginnings
of a good book, even a helpful book.
Finding time to write the stories became
an obsession with me because I knew
that as each year passed, my time to write and
publish was getting shorter and shorter.

I was fifty-eight years old when I held
In my hand that first book, loosely based on
some of my true memories. I could not
remember a more meaningful moment.

I had actually achieved my dream.
One book was not going to be enough.
I had many different stories that

perked through my brain awaiting the moment
when I would write them onto lined paper.

I have now passed my most recent goal of
twenty books so I'm going to have to
raise the bar again. I will continue
to write and, hopefully, my readers will
continue to take in all of my words.
I feel I must write and I will do so
until I can no longer clutch the pen.

Linda Hudson Hoagland

RIDING THE STORM

The Storm
of pestilence
called Covid

Many friends
all gone
riding Covid

Wait patiently
for vaccine
to survive

SEARCHING

Joseph Stevens became obsessive
for me when I received an email
with his name boldly attached to it.
It was just an e-mail. It was a
truly nice e-mail that made me smile
inside and out so I must meet him.

My search started on the computer.
It never occurred to me that so
many people might have the same name.
The computer displayed horrendous
totals of nearly fifty thousand
references to Joseph Stevens.

Doctors, authors, property-rental
owners, computer programmer-gamers,
a police officer from England.
What a group of educated men
to choose from to find Joseph Stevens.
In my fantasy world, he was all
of those things with a strong emphasis
on author. I always thought the mind
of a writer a worthwhile study.

To find out if the writer was my
Joseph Stevens, I decided I

needed to reach out to him and ask.
I found Joseph Stevens, Author, on
Amazon and I discovered that
he was a young man just starting out
in the world of writing. More power
to him in his future writing tasks.

Moving on. How about the doctor?
In his internet life, I found he
was a cardiologist living
in another state. His Facebook page was
permanently closed so there was no
way for me to reach him other
than making an appointment. I lived
nowhere near him— that was a no go.

Moving on, again. His work title
of Secure Systems Development
and Integration Engineer at
Metropolitan Police was much
longer than most careers. I could not
imagine he would take interest
in sending a nice e-mail to an
old lady. At almost sixty eight
put me in old lady category
in my mind. I didn't mind that so
much because I worked hard and earned those
years and the gray hair that came with it

Once more. Property owner— maybe.
I read Belfast as his location,
I was assuming that was Belfast,
Virginia. Boy, was I wrong. It
was in Belfast, United Kingdom
and that wasn't my Joseph Stevens.

It occurred to me if I hadn't
deleted the message, I might be
able to hit reply to see where
that would take me. Found it. Why I had
never deleted it was unknown.

When I hit send, I had my fingers
crossed. I was hoping for a rapid
response but— UNDELIVERABLE.

I was sorry I waited so long.

Linda Hudson Hoagland

SPRING

The flowers are
beginning to peep
through the cold
dark wet earth.

Spring is almost
here and I'm
anxiously waiting for
the sweet scents.

THE BEST GIFT

Valentine's Day was coming and I
didn't want to sink down into the
doldrums that led to depression and
feeling sorry for myself because
I don't have my Sonny to help me
celebrate. My sons had families
of their own demanding attention
and they were my only relatives.
My eldest son lived within ten miles
of my house but, for reasons unknown
to me, I was unwelcomed by his
wife to celebrate in their home. My
younger son resided nine hundred
miles away so visiting was out
of the question. I would usually
get a telephone call. My Sonny
died ten years earlier leaving me
a lonely, old widow who has cats:
two inside the house and two outside
with the addition, every so
often, of vagrant kitties in search
of food. Yes, I oblige. They get fed.
I had gotten to the point where I
knew I needed help and I asked God
and Sonny to help me get through the
holidays that I dreaded the most.

Christmas and New Year's came and went and
I didn't cry. That was much better
than I had done in the recent past.

I wasn't a person to expect
a gift for Valentine's Day but I
did get the best one I ever had.
I learned to smile at the mention of
Sonny's name and depression didn't
get to throw its sad cloak over me.

THE DRAFT

Was it the draft that caused my illness?
No, no, it was a germ, not the cool,
gentle breeze; but I was so sick and
there was no explanation. It was
the hundred-year pandemic and my
number came up. Let the cool, gentle
breeze carry me away with wings to
my peaceful forever and safe home.

Linda Hudson Hoagland

THE MOUNTAIN TOP

The mountain top was a great place to
while away the long hours of summer.
I spent many hours at Big Walker
Lookout selling the books I wrote and
the angel afghans I designed and
created. Then came the scourge of the
Covid and the world changed. The mountain
continued to be beautiful
but the people were mask covered and
scared. The few conversations that I
initiated to get them to
look at my books became bothersome
to the visitors at the Lookout.
Now, the people are returning but
the next big surge of the Covid is
building with hints of making us all
re-enter the world of masks again.
The mountain will remain beautiful.

THE MOVIE TICKETS

About a million times over
scheduled Saturdays, I have heard
the auctioneer chant as I worked as
clerk for a part time employer
and friend. I was on the business
side of the auction; therefore, I
wasn't able to join in on the
bidding process that could or could
not be a fantastic bargain.

This time it is different.
This time I get to play.
"The bid is ten; will anyone bid
twelve-fifty? Twelve-fifty? twelve-fifty,"
said the auctioneer as he looked around.

I raised my paddle to bid
twelve-fifty. "Twelve-fifty, twelve-fifty,
anybody want to make it
fifteen? Fifteen? Bid fifteen," he
said as he tried to urge those people
standing before him to meet his price.

"Sold for twelve-fifty," he said as the
young lady helping him handed
me an envelope containing twenty

dollars' worth of two movie tickets
that included the popcorn and
drinks at the movie house just down
the street from where I lived.
I was so proud of my purchase.
I knew Sonny would like to go to
the movies. It had been a long time
since we had enjoyed a movie.
Then, there was another pair of
tickets for a movie theater
about fifteen miles from us held
up for bid. I got both tickets for
seven-fifty. That's the price of
one ticket alone. Now we can go
to the movies twice and enjoy life.
I could hardly wait to tell him.

The only reason I am here
bidding on things I don't need is
that Tammy asked me to help with
the auction fundraiser for the
Parent Teacher Association
at the small school where she is the
secretary and the mother of
two young children who attend the school.

I didn't have the money to
waste but I did it anyway.
Most people I speak with do not

consider early sixties as
waning years, but with Sonny and his
bad heart, tomorrow could be his
last day or perhaps even today.

I tucked the tickets away into
my purse to wait for a movie
to appear on the screen that we
really wanted to see. I was
planning to use the tickets during
the coming holiday season.

Driving to a movie theater
will give us a chance to go out
and see all the lights that will be
shining from many of the homes in
our small town. I made the purchase
on Saturday in late October.

Sonny went to the hospital
on Tuesday for a colon test that
was performed on Wednesday. That very
same Wednesday, Sonny went into
a coma. He never woke up.

Now, I guess I will give those tickets
to Michael, my son, and Donna,
his girlfriend. Hopefully, they will
enjoy going to the movies
over the lonely holidays.

I don't think I can do it now.

THE PEACH

Its soft fuzz
beneath my fingers
let's me think
of the sweet
succulent great taste
of pure goodness.

When I cut
into the flesh,
I feel the
juices run down
my fingers and
I can't wait
to finally eat.

Linda Hudson Hoagland

THE PEARLS

I drove slowly onto the graveled lane
leading me to my lonely, darkened house
never suspecting the awaiting pain.
All inside was as quiet as a mouse.

The door standing ajar and that I knew
was a sign of something so very bad.
Why it happened to me, I had no clue.
Many of my things by others were had.

The small box that held my grandmother's pearls
was no longer found on the old dresser.
The blankets were thrown on the floor in curls.
The pearls, I'm no longer the possessor.

If I could place a bad curse on the strand,
I'd want to place the pearls in the thief's hand.

THE RIGHT THING

My lawyer daddy was raising my
brother and me in Alabama
during the depression. Things were so
different because not all people
were treated the same. If your skin was
dark, you weren't treated like the white folks.
We had playmates with that darker skin
and the only thing I could see that
was different about them was skin
color. My friends weren't allowed to go
to the same school I went to or they
didn't go at all. My daddy, the
lawyer, decided to take a case
defending a man of color. That
seemed to be a mistake as far as
our neighbors were concerned. It was thought
the black man shouldn't be defended;
instead, he should be taken out to the
nearest tall tree and hanged by the neck
until dead. My daddy said the black
man didn't rape the white girl and it
was my daddy's job to prove that the
accused black man was not the rapist.
People were really angry with my
daddy and decided the best way
to get back at him was to kill us:

my brother and me. A man with the
darker skin saved my brother and me
from being killed by a crazy man.

Even though things did not work out like
my daddy wanted it to go, he
felt he had done the right thing.

He did this at a time when things like this were
not accepted in To Kill A Mockingbird.

TIME SLITHERS

No matter what we do, time grows limp with
dehydration of the juices of life.

It wilts into a weak memory, then
slithers away to be rejuvenated into
a new beginning.

Trees reach to the summit of growing;
furniture becomes scratched and weak with use;
and mankind reaches the end to be recycled.

TO BE FREE

I find myself just smiling
a lot more these at home days.
I've earned my easy living
through many work-a-day stays.

I smile because I get to
do only what I choose so
now I have much more to do,
so off to living I go.

I have volunteered my time
to those who will need it most
to fill up the hours sometime
and not feel that I must boast.

I give my service to each,
making many friends each day,
To chase away blues, I reach
for something to do I pray.

I will continue to be
happy as long as I can
be of use to those I see.
Make the most of life, I plan.

Retirement is what you make
of it. Come join me and see.
Life can be something to take
and enjoy it, to be free.

WITH SONNY – I GOT IT RIGHT

After two errors in judgement
I'm not seeking another.
His sparkling blue eyes and broad smile
Pushed me to consider the other.

I tried to find a way to ask
For his company and friendship
Without being too obvious.
Being forward was a hardship.

My excited son called to say
That a snake was under our house.
I called Sonny for help to kill
A snake, not a little gray mouse.

He thought the excuse was funny
For him to drop in and help me,
But come he did and he did stay
Thus ending his eternity.

WRITER'S DAY

Overcast day.
Table sitting.
Selling books.

I write it.
You buy it.

Clutched pen.
Written words.
Good enough?

My life spread
On these pages.

Heart exposed.
Paper story.
Please read.

WRONG DECISION

It was my hope to find a new home
in a different state to keep my
tween sons away from the enticements
of trouble. Over their multiple
objections, we moved to a rural
area where the drugs and mischief
weren't invading. Instead, my eldest
son was struck by a car— wrong decision.

ACKNOWLEDGMENTS

Star Poets – "A Nice Young Man"

Star Poets – "A Voyeur's Look"

Northern Stars – "Addie"

Golden Nib – "Alone"

Northern Stars & Star Poets – "Alzheimer"

Star Poets – "Appalachian Fun"

Star Poets – "Book 13"

Front Porch Monthly – "Call of Kindness"

The Weekly Avocet – "Dive!"

Northern Stars – "Ed – Father of My Sons"

The Bluestone Review & Star Poets – "Flag of Freedom"

Avantappal Ezine – "Frigid Full Moon"

Star Poets – "Grandma Wishes"

Star Poets – "Gray Crowned Angels"

Star Poets – "Happy Hello"

Star Poets – "Homeless"

Star Poets – "I Adored Mr. Lace"

Northern Stars – "I Am an Author"

Star Poets – "I Finally Got It Right"

Virginia Writers Club Journal 2023 – "I will Always Remember"

Star Poets – "Joe – My Work Love"

Star Poets – "John – My Dangerous Love"

Star Poets – "Justice"

Northern Stars – "Leaves Tumble"

Northern Stars – "Live"

Star Poets – "Maybe"

Northern Stars – "Meeting and Greeting"

Star Poets – "Mike – My Second Attempt"

Avantappal Ezine & Star Poets & Northsouthappalachia Blogspot – "Mud Tracks"

Front Porch Monthly – "My Bad"
Northern Stars & Star Poets – "My Big Brother"
Star Poets – "My Card"
Northern Stars & Star Poets – "My Husband – My Hero"
Star Poets – My Secret Trip"
Clinch Mountain Review & Northern Stars – "Neighbor
    Envy"
Front Porch Monthly – "Not in Our Bed"
*The Bluestone Review & Clinch Mountain Review & Star
    Poets* – "Old"
Star Poets – "Panic"
Star Poets – "Proud Peacock"
Star Poets – "Published Opines"
Star Poets - "Raising the Bar Again"
The Bluestone Review & Star Poets – "Riding the Storm"
Northern Stars – "Searching"
Northern Stars – "Spring"
Star Poets - "Still My Friend"
Star Poets & The Howl – "Thankful"
Northern Stars – "The Best Gift"
Star Poets – "The Draft"
*Clinch Mountain Review & Northern Stars &
Northsouthappalachia Blog Spot* – "The Mountain Top"
Northern Stars – "The Movie Tickets"
Northern Stars – "The Peach"
Northern Stars – "The Pearls"
Star Poets & Poetry Society of Tennessee – "The Right
    Thing"
Avantappal Ezine – "Time Slithers"
Northern Stars – "To Be Free"
Northern Stars – "With Sonny I Got It Right"
Star Poets - "Writer's Day"
Northern Stars – "Wrong Decision"

The Mountain Top and other poems

ABOUT THE AUTHOR

Linda Hudson Hoagland of Tazewell, Virginia, a graduate of Southwest Virginia Community College, has won acclaim for many of her novels that include *Snooping Can Be Dangerous, Snooping Can Be Contagious, Snooping Can Be Devious, Snooping Can Be Doggone Deadly, Snooping Can Be Helpful – Sometimes, Snooping Can Be Uncomfortable, Snooping Can Be Scary, Snooping Can Be Regrettable. The Best Darn Secret, Onward & Upward,* and *Missing Sammy,* all published by Jan-Carol Publishing, Inc.

Other publications include: *Dangerous Shadow, Crooked Road Stalker, Checking on the House, Death By Computer, The Backwards House, An Awfully Lonely Place,* and *An Unjust Court* from Hoot Books Publishing.

Hoagland has written other fiction, nonfiction, poetry, and short stories that have been included in many anthologies, including *Broken Petals, Easter Lilies, Wild Daisies, Scattered Flowers, Daffodil Dreams, Snowy Trails* and *These Haunted Hills Books 1-5,* and several more.

Hoagland is a retired Tazewell County Schools System employee, where she worked as a purchase order clerk for almost 23 years. She is a proud mother of two sons.

OTHER BOOKS WRITTEN BY LINDA HUDSON HOAGLAND:

<u>FICTION</u>

SNOOPING CAN BE UN-MERRY

SNOOPING CAN BE REGRETTABLE

SNOOPING CAN BE SCARY

SNOOPING CAN BE UNCOMFORTABLE

SNOOPING CAN BE HELPFUL - SOMETIMES

SNOOPING CAN BE DOGGONE DEADLY

SNOOPING CAN BE DEVIOUS

SNOOPING AND BE CONTAGIOUS

SNOOPING CAN BE DANGEROUS

THE BEST DARN SECRET

DANGEROUS SHADOW

ONWARD & UPWARD

AN UNJUST COURT

CROOKED ROAD STALKER

CHECKING ON THE HOUSE

DEATH BY COMPUTER

THE BACKWARDS HOUSE

AN AWFULLY LONELY PLACE

NONFICTION

LIVE A LITTLE

LEARN A LOT

LIVING A LIFE

MISSING SAMMY

MY FIRST 90 YEARS

QUILTED MEMORIES

A GUITAR, A BIBLE AND A SHOTGUN

WATCH OUT FOR EDDY

JUST A COUNTRY BOY: DON DUNFORD

THE LITTLE OLD LADY NEXT DOOR (Out of Print)

COLLECTIONS

THE TRUTH IS... AND OTHER STORIES

WHAT WAS THAT? AND OTHER STORIES

FRANK'S FATE & OTHER STORIES

A COLLECTION OF WINNERS

A COLLECTION OF WINNERS 2

THE MOUNTAIN TOP AND OTHER POEMS

THE CUP AND OTHER POEMS

THE LAST TIME & OTHER POEMS

ANGELS TO WOMEN OF THE WORLD - POETRY

I AM...LINDA ELLEN - POETRY

ANTHOLOGIES

DAFFODIL DREAMS

SCATTERED FLOWERS

WILD DAISIES

SEASONS OF OUR LIVES - AUTUMN

MOUNTAIN MIST

MOUNTAIN VOICES

THESE HAUNTED HILLS BOOK 1 - 5

EASTER LILIES

BROKEN PETALS

CHRISTMAS BLOOMS (Out of Print)

CUP OF COMFORT FOR A BETTER WORLD

AND MORE TITLES BY REQUEST

**Visit my website for books you want personalized:
lindasbooksandangels.co**

Made in the USA
Columbia, SC
04 October 2024

43024172R00050